Like Mushrooms

Alex McGilvery

ISBN 978-1-989092-52-1

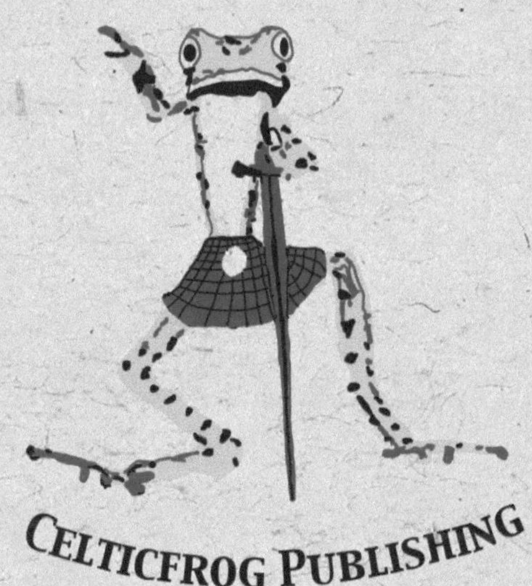

CELTICFROG PUBLISHING

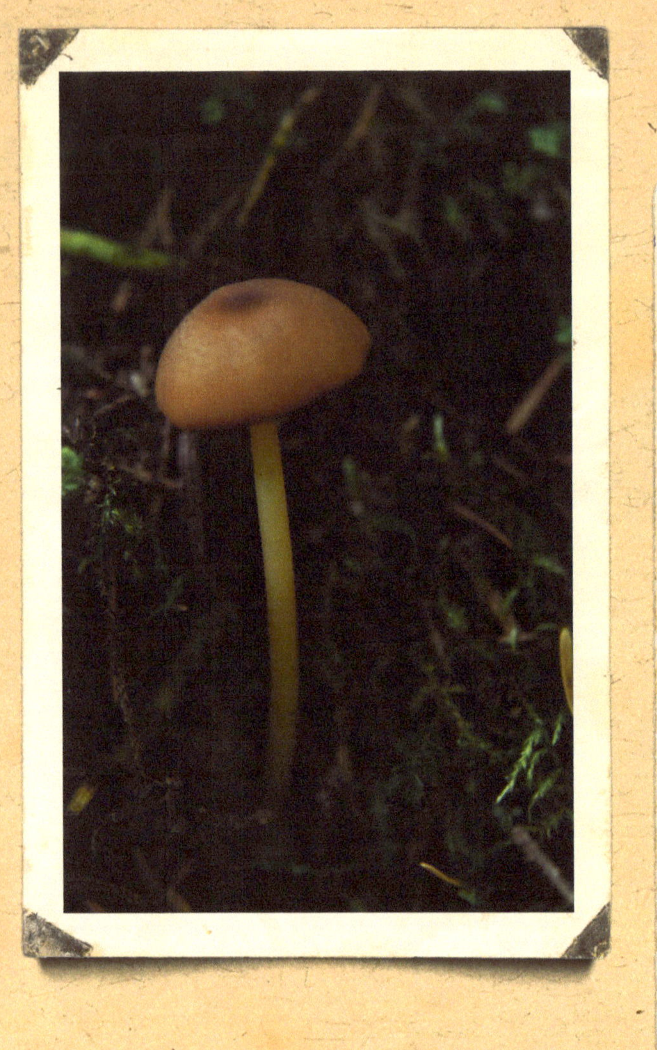
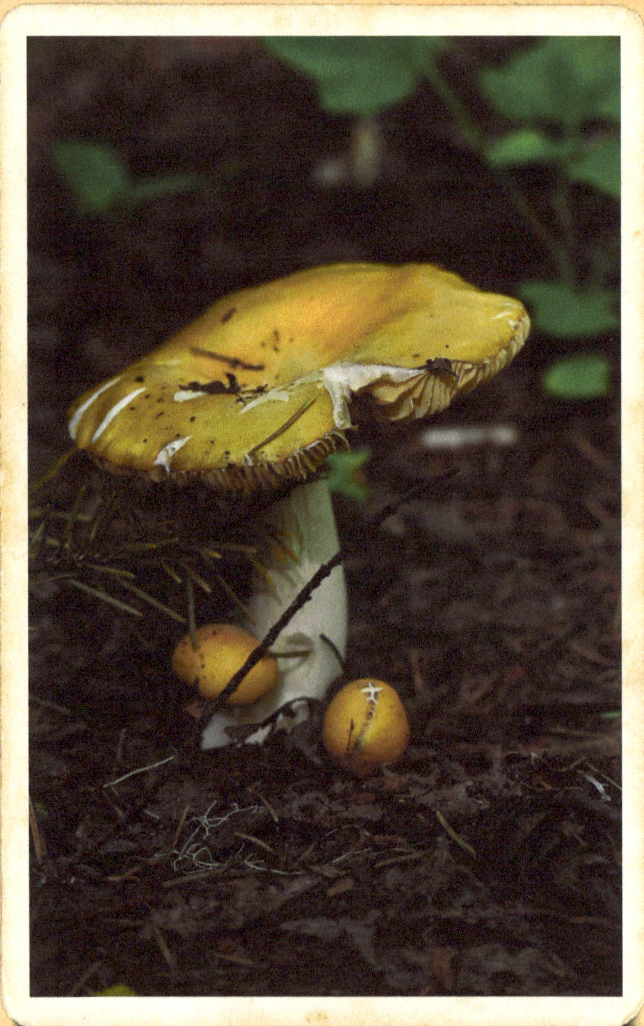

Like Mushrooms

Like mushrooms, they sprout in places of decay,
Some deadly poison, others
sliding over the tongue
Like butter and garlic

They compost dead things into the soil of new life
Or hang wooden on a trunk,
A sign of rot at the core
Waiting to become art.

Invisible mycelium joins us
Beneath the surface
We are connected
In ways we can't imagine

Like mushrooms they come
After the rains
Colourful reminders in their profusion
Even here is life.

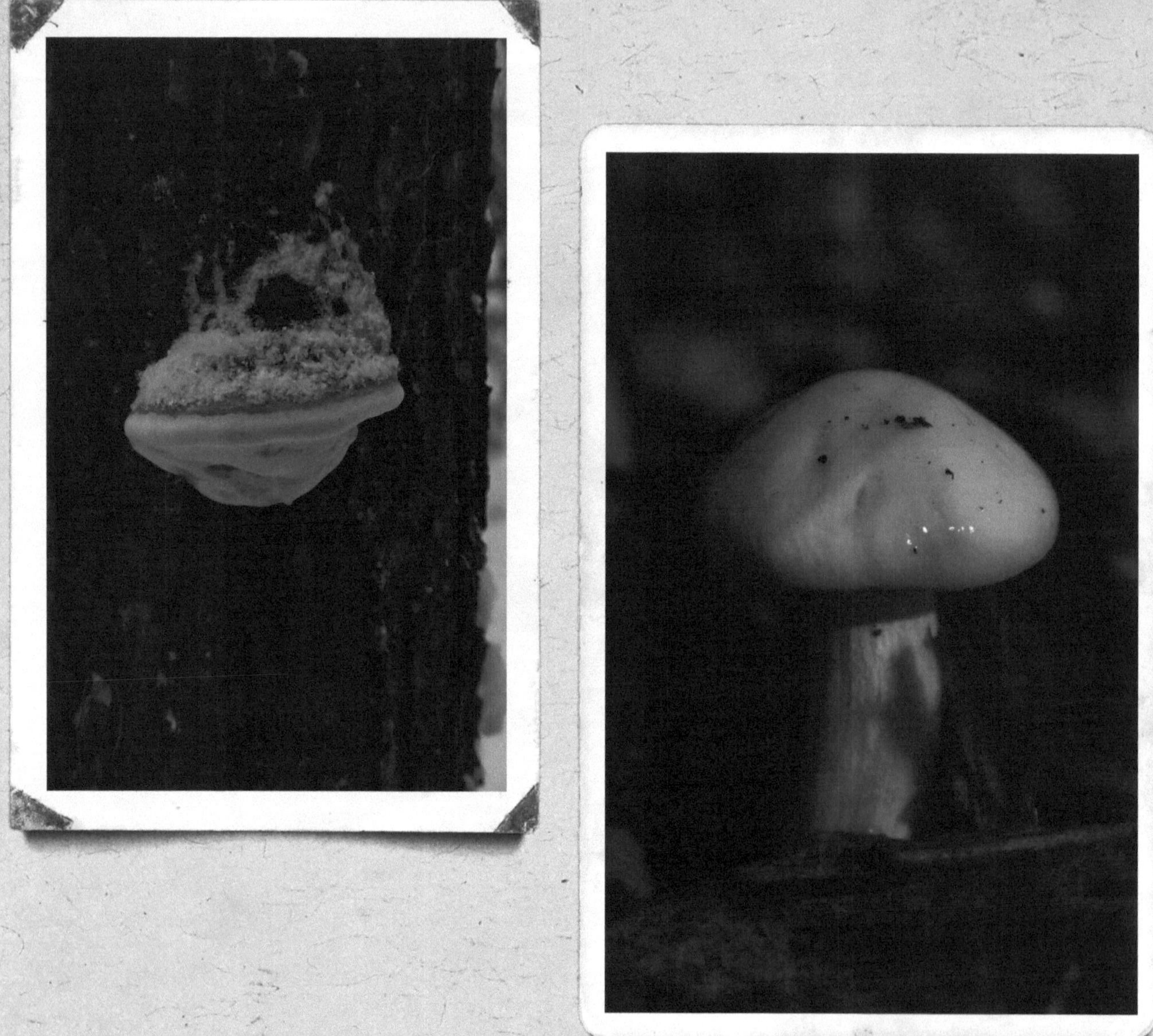

Nocturnal creatures, these mindless worms
made from equal parts
half-remembered music and old regrets.
Slithering through my soul
leaving the slime of unspeakable notions,
or what I might have said
to some long ago bully.

Sleep is a dystopian story–
Dreams of violence or Greek tragedy
disturb and disorder until,
yet again, I'm wakened by an
uncountered left hook.

Sitting up to rub imaginary bruises,
relief brings me, ambulatory,
to the light of refrigerator
or screen, where I may
produce or consume what
sweetness needed to send the worms
to sleep.
In hope, I may, in time, follow.

The detritus of my night –
wrack and ruin of ideas,
unspoken dialogues,
the taste of old fear,
accompanies my waking.
Day begins by brushing off the remains,
shaking the silvered trails
from my pillow.

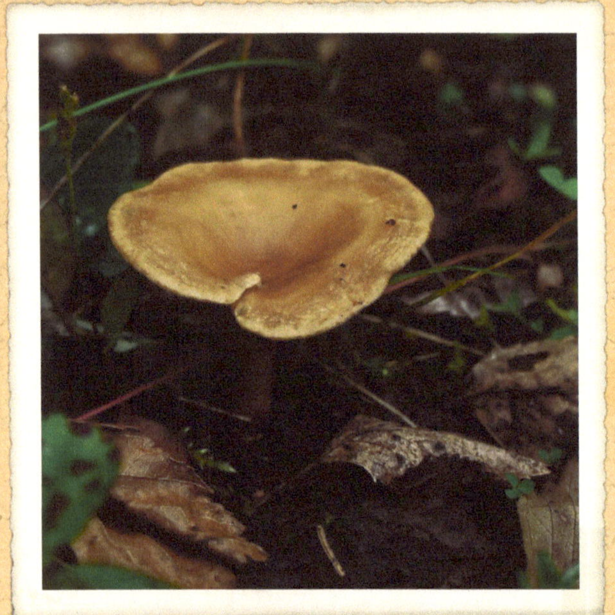

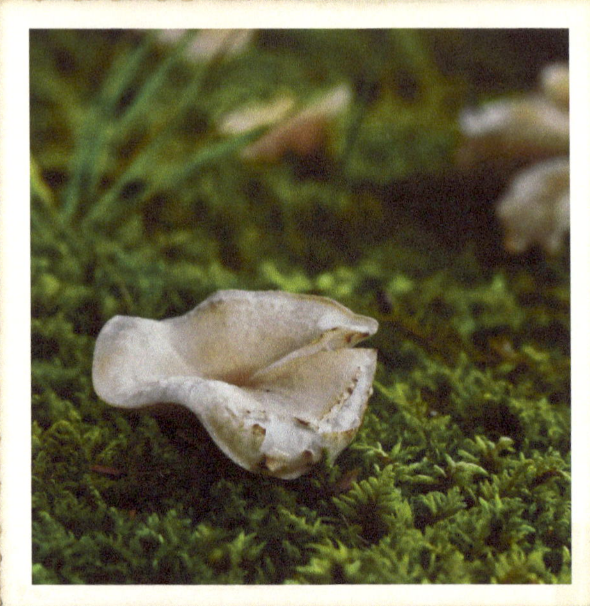

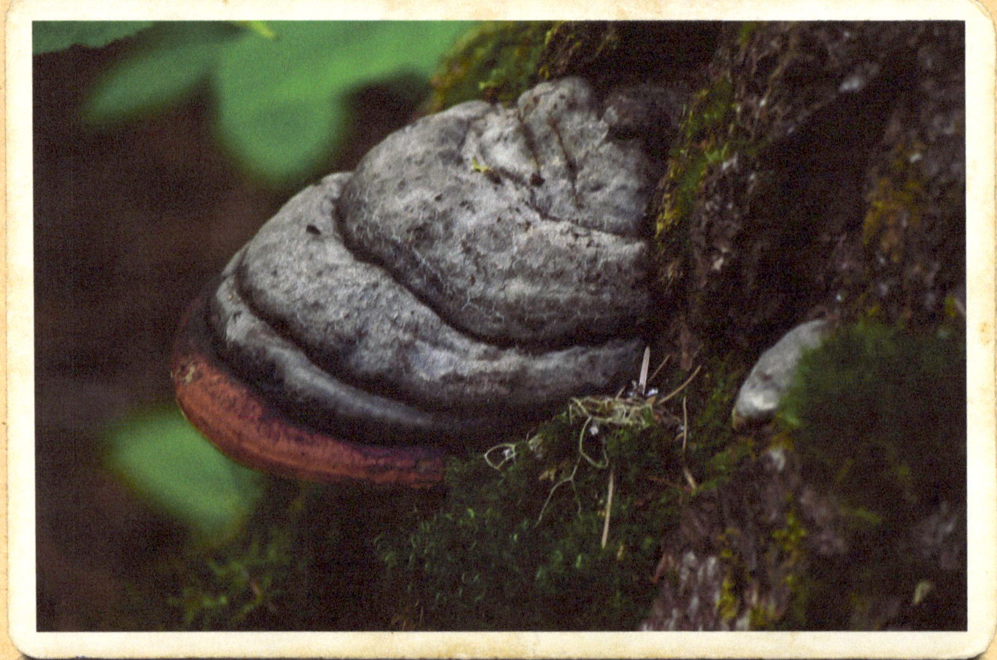

Nails

Metal ravaged from rock by red hot flue
Red iron hammered thin and square; cooling black
Nails hold tight to ancient wood when set true
Driven by small blows or one mighty whack

Red iron hammered thin and square; cooling black
Now set hot to hoof to anchor a shoe
Driven by small blows or one mighty whack
Horses run over rocks or mud like glue

Now set hot to hoof to anchor a shoe
Carrying warriors to battle their foe
Horses run over rocks or mud like glue
Where loss of nail or shoe or horse brings woe

Carrying warriors to battle their foe
Courage isn't enough when numbers fail
Where loss of nail or shoe or horse brings woe
Victorious or defeated the widows wail

Courage isn't enough when numbers fail
Men stumble home to tally the cost
Victorious or defeated the widows wail
Crooked, broken, forgotten and lost

Men stumble home to tally the cost
Time has its way, even iron will rust
Crooked, broken, forgotten and lost
All our life's work from is just so much dust.

Time has its way even iron will rust
Metal ravaged from rock by red hot flue
All our life's work yield is just so much dust.
Nails hold tight to ancient wood when set true

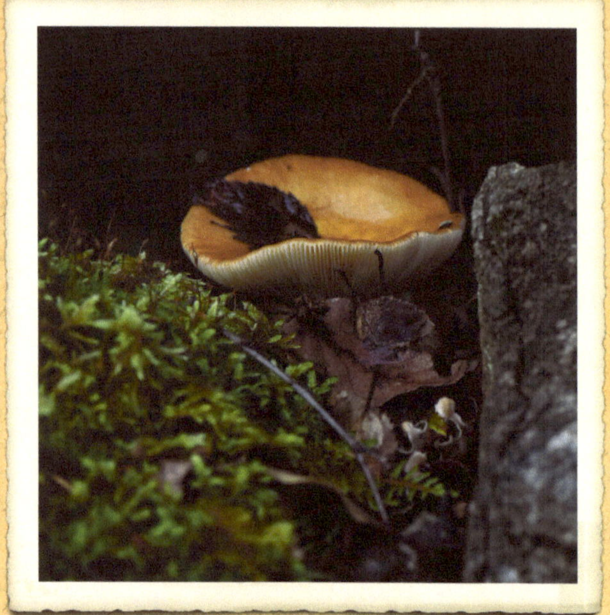

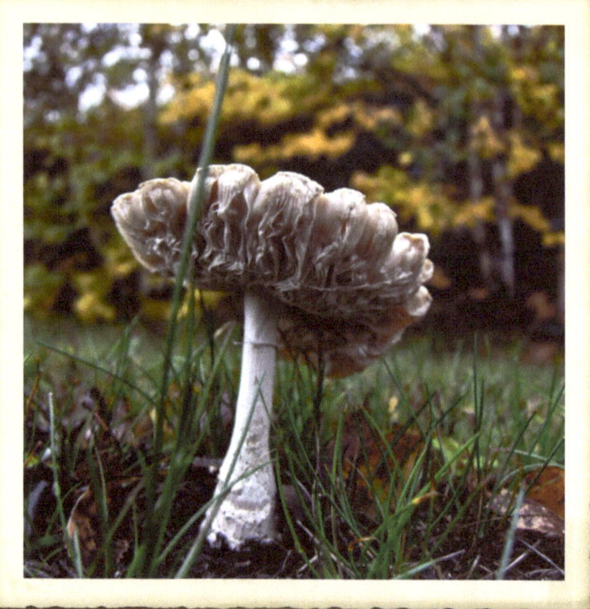

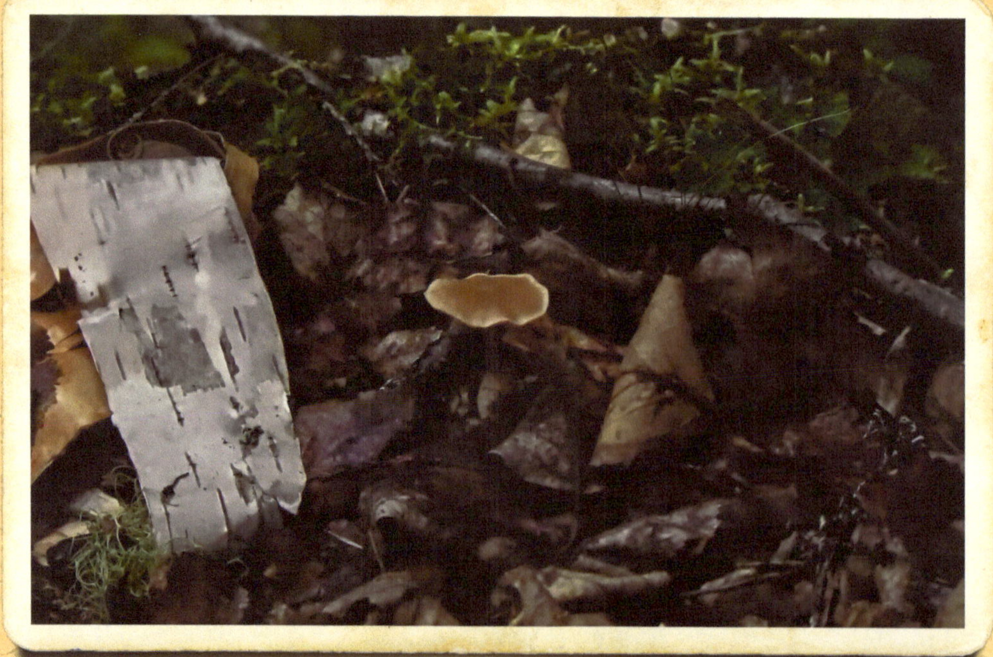

Fire

Flames reach far into the sky,
Trees explode like popcorn
A hundred miles away people cough in the smoke
Airplanes drop bombs of water.
Men and women with ashen faces dig trenches
and pray for rain.

The forest needs fire for renewal,
Death is necessary for life.
Between blackened trunks, blueberries grow to fatten bears.
Spring comes out of season
New forest grows through the bones of the old.

There will always be rock
There will always be fire
What will grow between our dusty bones is yet unknown.
We grow in the soil of our ancestors,
Though our children may choke on the ash of our passing

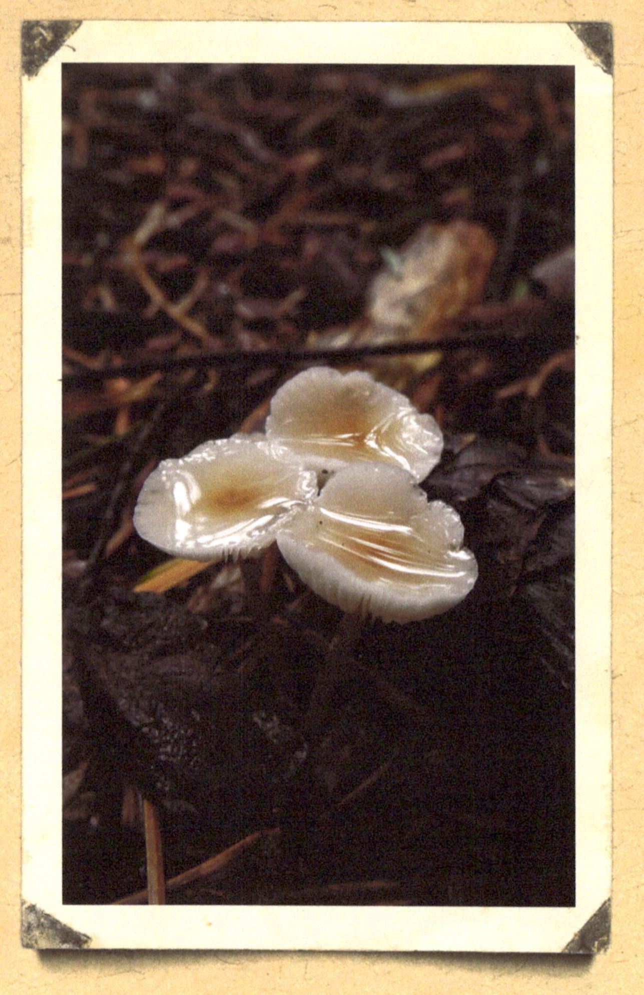
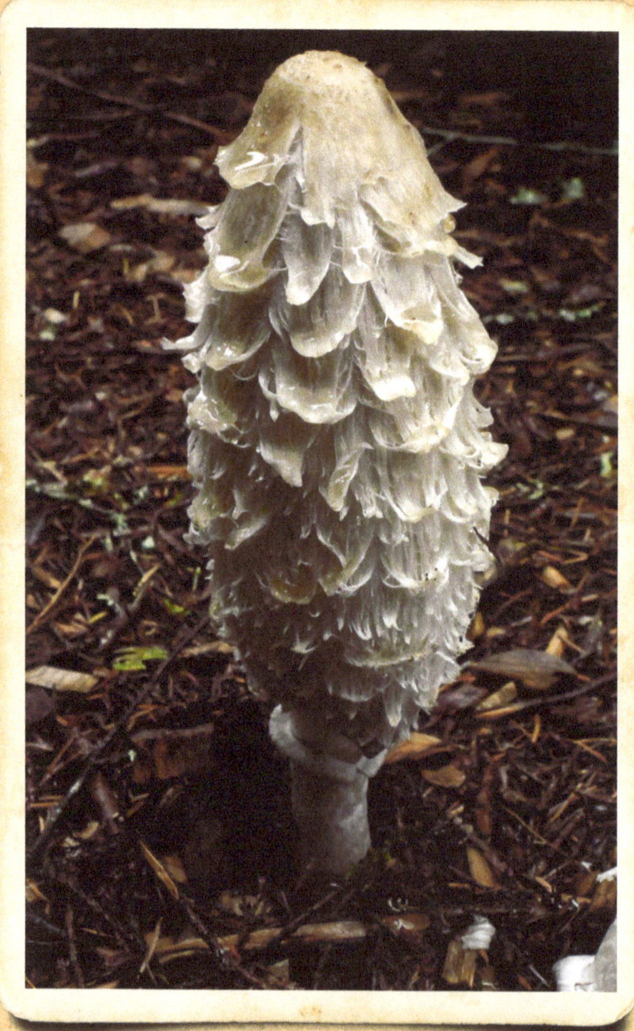

Fences

They wander the night streets in hordes
revelling in the physical
wrestling, punching, kissing
dragging on cigarettes and cheap beer
occasionally they shout insult
or smash a fence
and like coward monkeys flee into the dark.

They live by a code more rigid
resisting the law of their elders
fighting, hating, loving
meeting friends at court to tell
how weary judges threaten them with
a barbed wire fence
to return with blue triumph under their skin.

Will they age to wait up too late
worrying over their children
ranting, hoping, loving
sipping on single malt with ice
perhaps to consider in neutral tones
mending fences
yet sigh and shield their young from consequence?

We live our live in this moment
seeing no aerial view
knowing, learning, trusting
bleeding for wrongs done and received
to reach with glorious courage
over the fences
to touch another's life with hope.

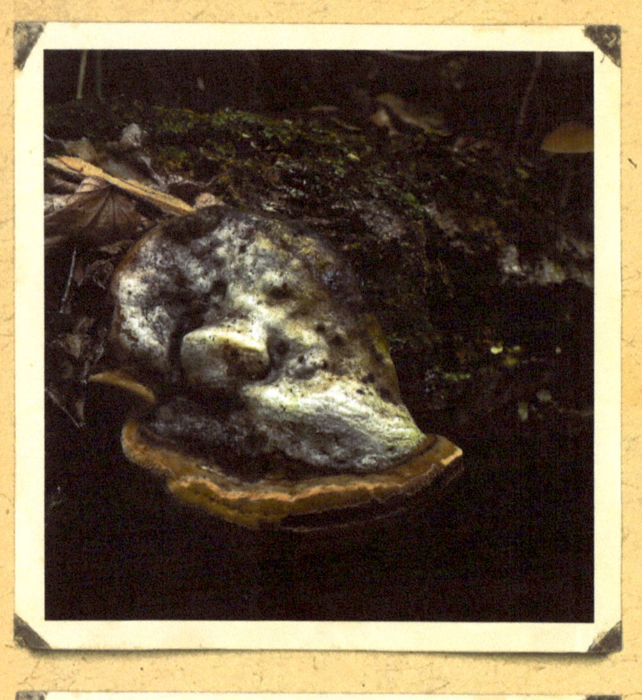

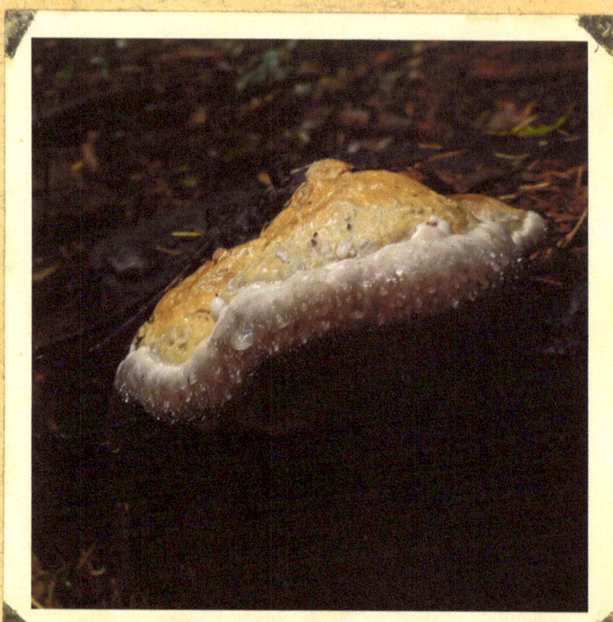

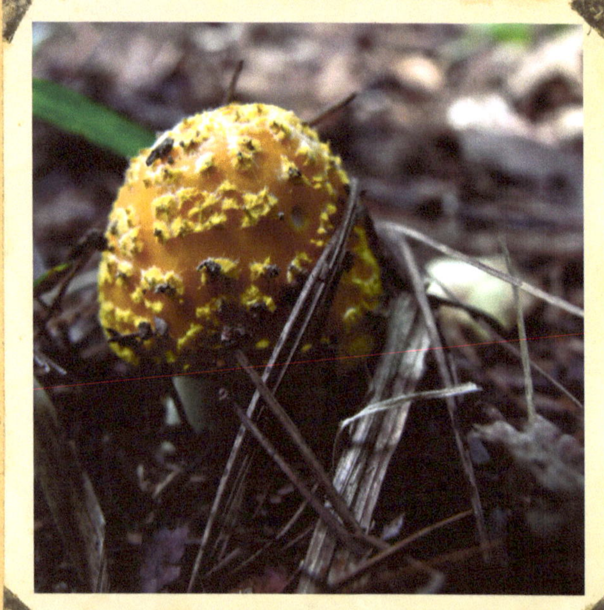

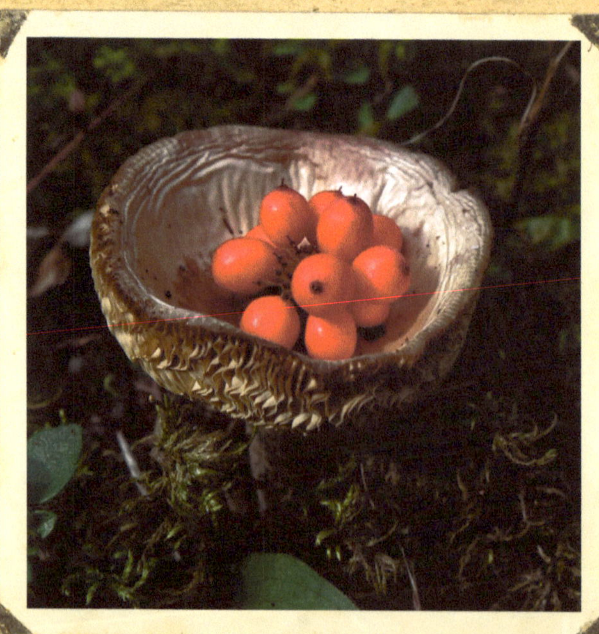

Fragments of Fragile Minds

A ghost haunting my own life,
I limp through the fog.
So far from myself,
if you stab me with a pin,
a doll somewhere will scream.

I knew a woman, who
even in the last of her days
sat straight with dignity.
She published books of poems in her prime.
Now her son reads from the book
her name on the cover.
Tears leak from her eyes.
"I wish I could write poems like that."

A man drank his mind away.
He'd phone once a day,
five times, a dozen.
Words like ants swarmed out of him,
Until they ate him from the inside out
Leaving only the skeleton of his addiction.
Yet in his dissolution he
accomplished his dream.

This poem is trying to write me.
Something about holes in my mind
words falling to shatter
as glass on the ground.
I do not rhyme nor walk in meter.
In disgust the poem stalks off
Leaving only the taste of old words on my lips.

A Quilt of Nights

Trees blush green at their nakedness
in the dim light of evening.
Far above the crescent moon
geese honk mournfully searching, like we do,
for a nice lakefront home.
Stars peek out, forming patterns to shape our course.
Their faint light recalls the springtime of our world.
Already travelled through aeons to illuminate
the nighttime of creatures whose grief
is etched in the rock, damp beneath the blanket.
There we make our own light to answer the stars
They wheel above as we below.
Until scented with burgeoning life,
the night breeze accompanies us home.

***

Sun-warmed rocks hold us while
pungent repellent cologne
creates a fragile bubble
almost free of mosquitoes.
We lie still but for occasional smacks
as biters find sensitive parts
Bats flit, feasting on bloody pests,
Vampires at one remove.
Silent ghost, an owl seizes its meal
The circle widens, we feed the night.
Above terrestrial life and death
the Milky Way pours starlight
into our souls, feeding us
as we feed mosquitoes and bats and owls.
In the distance loons laugh.
Even as we flee homeward
pieces of us remain to flit and feed
and die.

Last glow of setting sun lights
the fire of the autumn trees.
Frost rims the grass;
flowers have become withered husks.
Chill air warns - all heat fades.
Even stars die whimpering or screaming
to spread the dust of their life
as far as our huddled bodies.
Meteors fling themselves through
The firmament adding their mass
To the earth's spin.
Creatures rustle,
Risking death to store life.
Elk trumpet calling each to each
To battle and to love.

***

Icy snow steals heat from our layered forms.
Green fire prances above.
Dimming stars,
giving Orion a cerulean cloak
to blow in cosmic wind
What we lose in warmth,
we gain in awe open mouthed, frozen tongued.
at the aurora's great dance.
The hiss may be our frosted breath,
or slippers of another world
sliding across the sky
Though trees are bare sticks
or stark black spikes against the colour swept heavens,
as if we wore Oz's glasses
all is lit in emerald shades.
We force our eyes to look away.
Back in shivering bodies
we retreat to warmth and sleep,
To dream of celestial song.

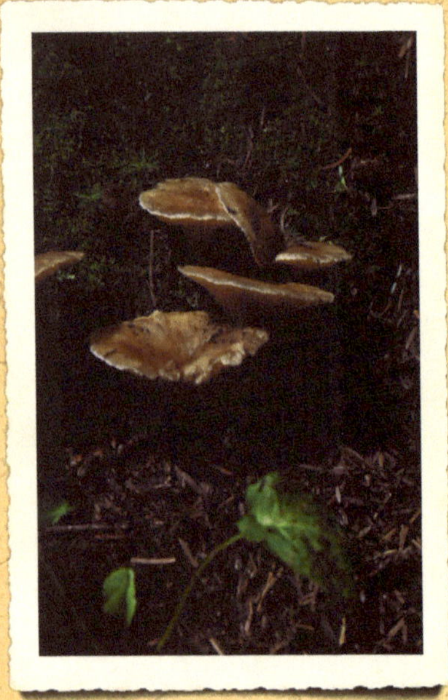
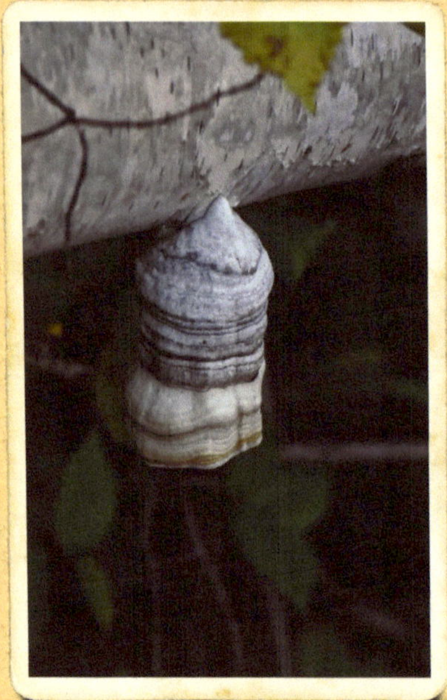
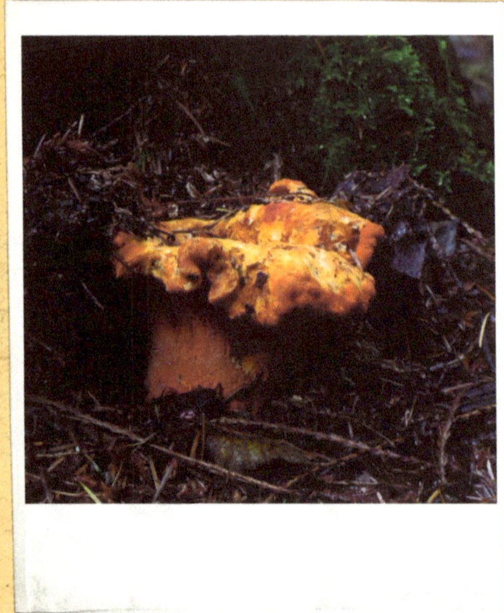
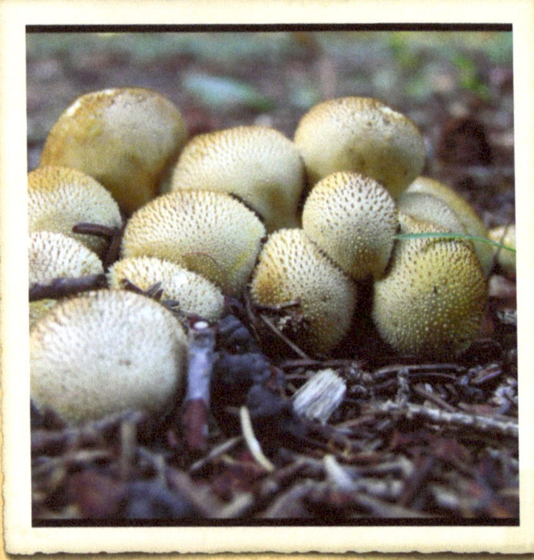
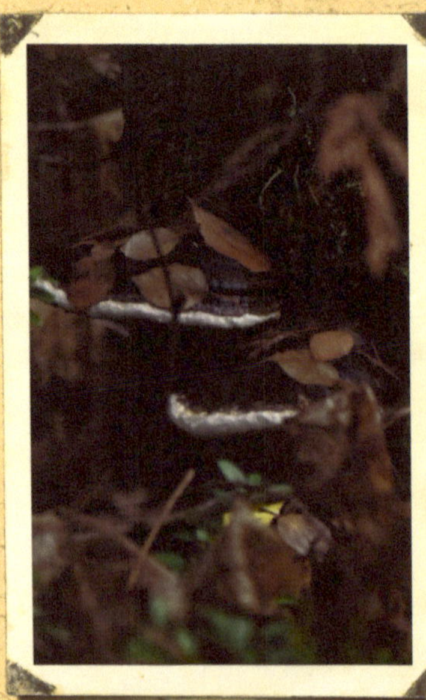
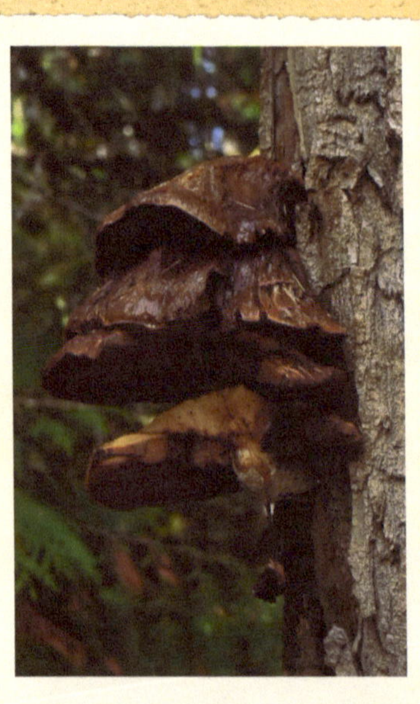

Green

Tendrils climb through rich black soil,
Leaves stretch up to warmth of sun,
Buds burst bright green unfolding
Deep shade on forest floor below.

Whether flow'r or tree all reach high,
To strive for light, seeking air,
Wresting space to grow and bloom.
Twisting, tangling, to live or die.

No peaceful wooded Eden here.
Enemies in shades of green.
Survival, not by beauty,
But nature green in root and branch.

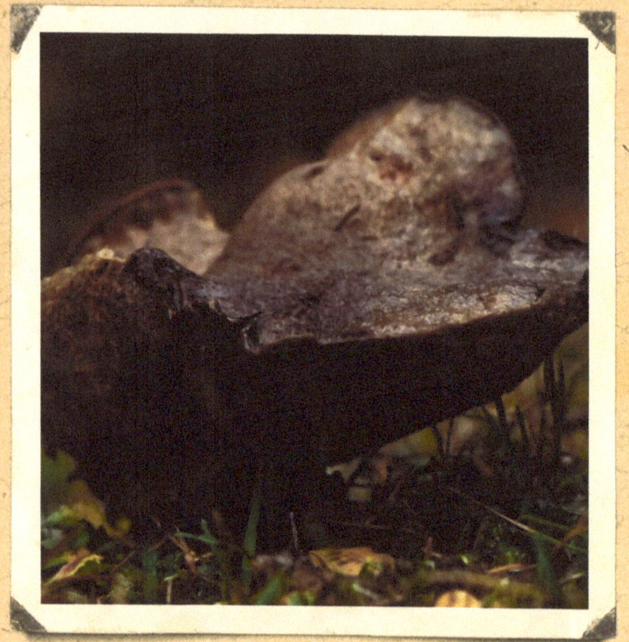
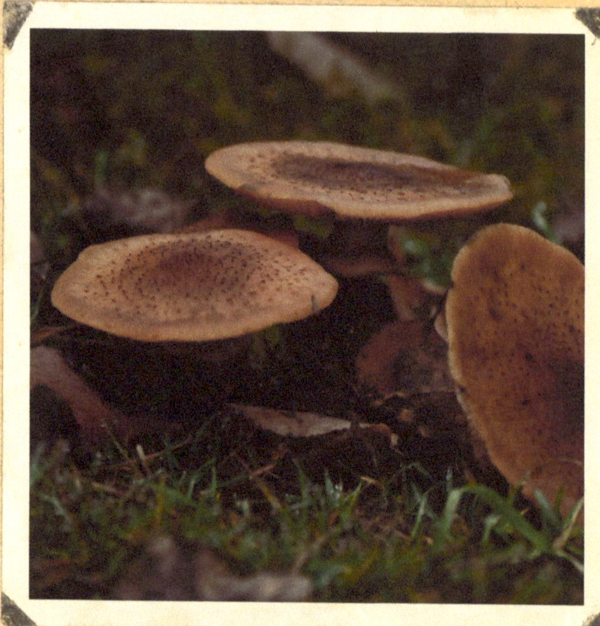
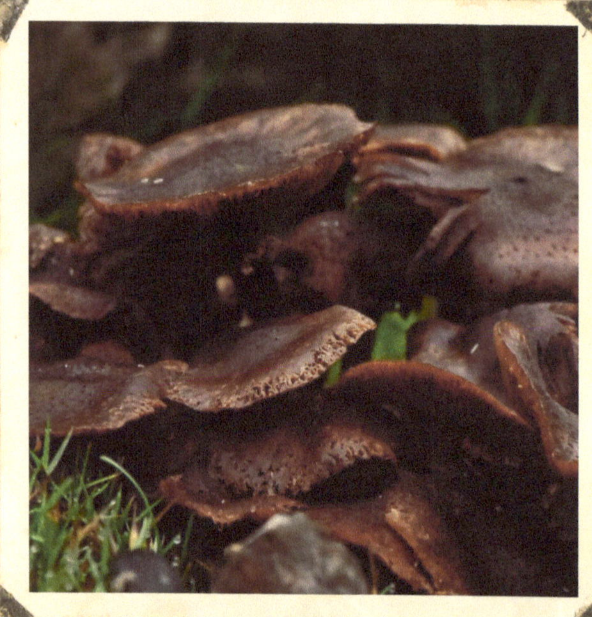
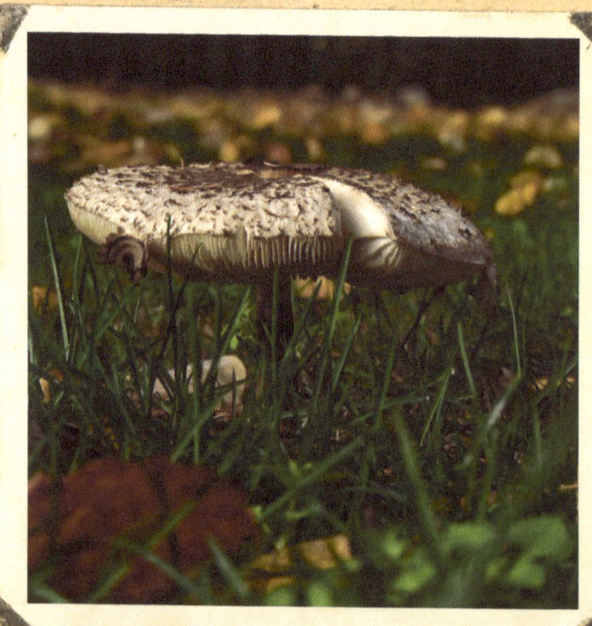

If hearts were made of wood.

If hearts were made of wood,
mine would be oak
solid, strong, heavy, prone to splitting
when dropped on rocks and kicked
further down the road when,
clumsy, I try to pick it up.

If hearts were made of wood
mine would be broken, see, places where,
glued together, the grain doesn't quite match
from times of careless rage, unthinking of the value of hearts
we threw them at each other to shatter against walls we built.
then penitent, we picked up pieces to glue them in place.
I got a piece of yours, lighter,
scented like forest with dappled light between deep shadows

If hearts were made of wood
mine is polished by oils from fingers risking splinters
to smooth away abrasions by rock and brick and word.
my hands have splinters, shards of you which catch and ache
too deep to remove by blade or needle
they remain part of me

If hearts were made of wood
Mine has been lost in rubble, smashed pieces of walls, hopes,
dreams broken and fulfilled, found, smoothed, cherished
even with still rough edges and fresh splinters in need of repair
hoping to be rejoined

If hearts were made of wood
mine would be a meld of oak and cedar.
carved with runes telling stories
as fingers brush against them saying do you remember?
I do

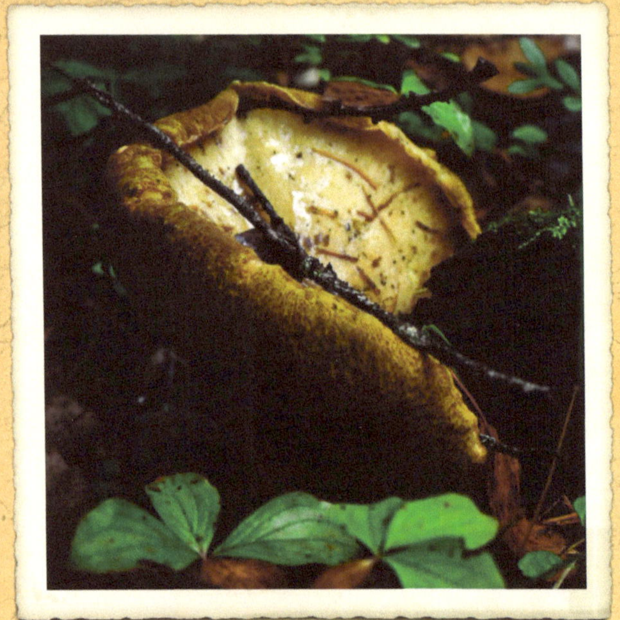

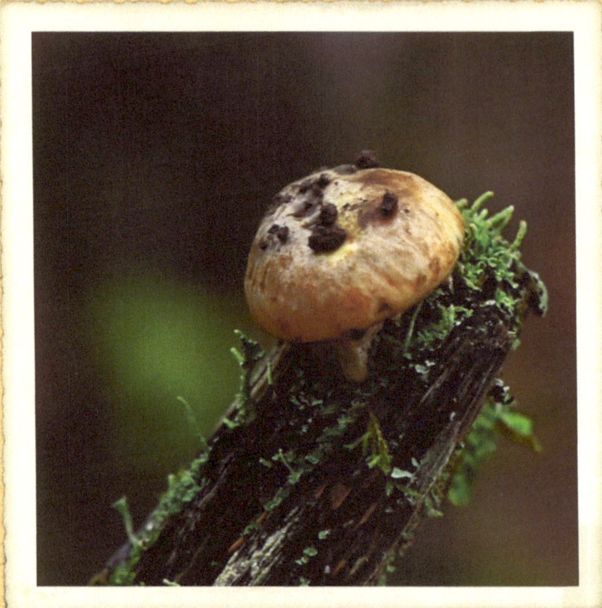

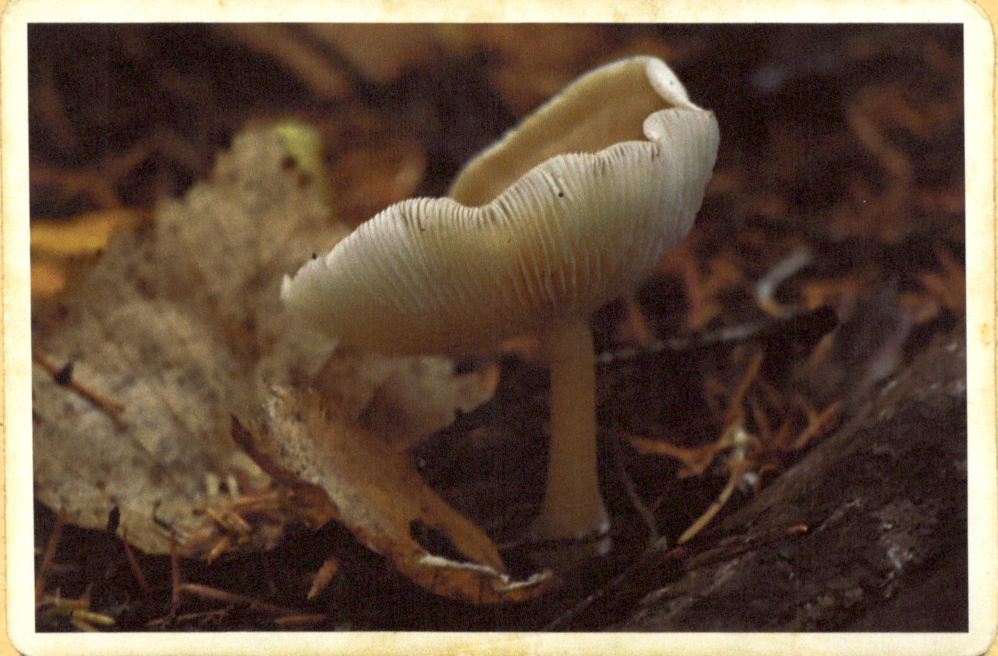

The Mirror Lies

The mirror lies
It shows me whole when I know
I lie in fractures pieces conquered
by the miseries of life.

The mirror lies
I see calm determination when
voices wail in lament within my mind
fearful of what is to come

The mirror lies
It show eyes like calm pools yet
my soul is troubled like the ocean
swells before the storm.

The mirror lies
yet I will believe its falsehood since
it shows a deeper truth – battered
I still stand before it

Broken, lamenting, troubled I
am shown a reflection of me that
is not all of what I may be.
the mirror lies.

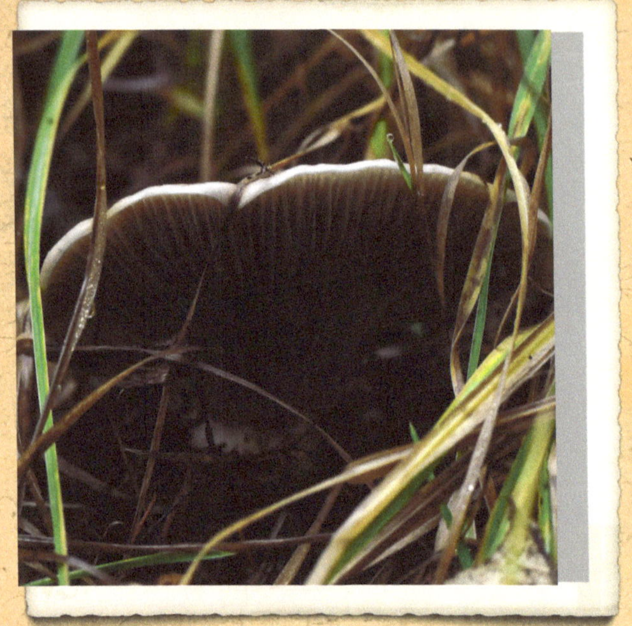
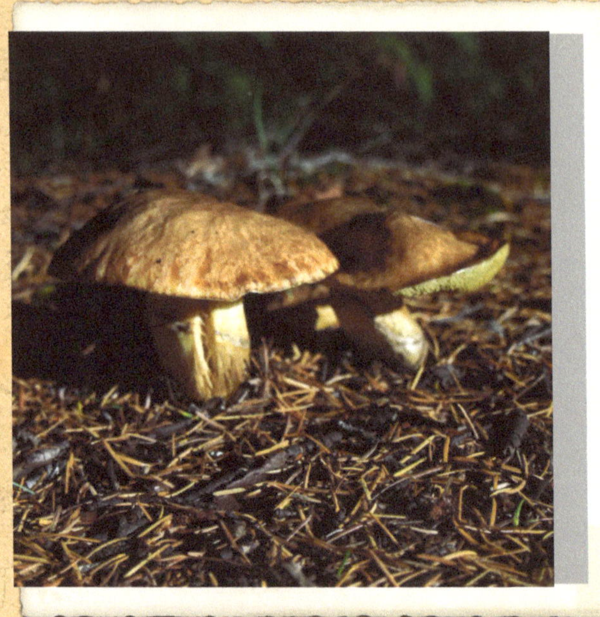
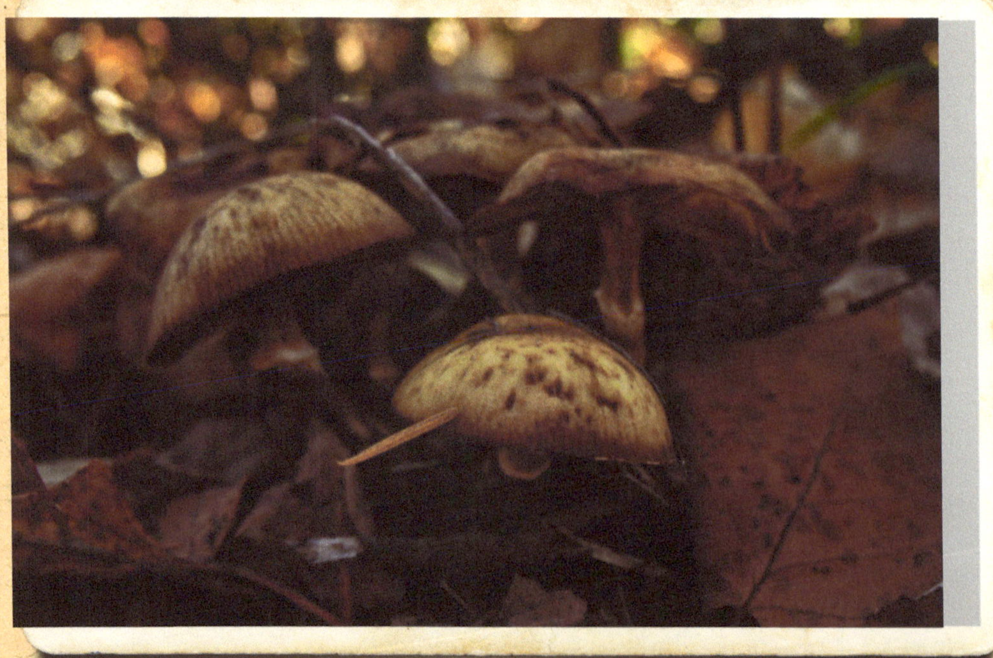

Hamster

All day the hamster sleeps
Lazy under its bed of shavings
Even food rates a bare twitch of the nose
Extreme sleeper, the nap is strong with this one.

At night the beast wakens
Leaping maniacally about the cage
Enters the hamster wheel shrieking
Excited to go nowhere at high speed

Again the hamster sleeps
Leaving its midnight furies
Even breaths make shavings tremble
Except the wheel is still squeaking.

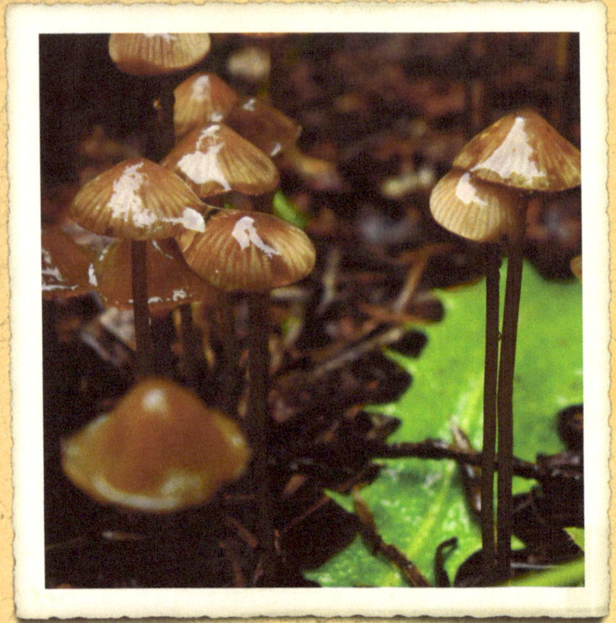

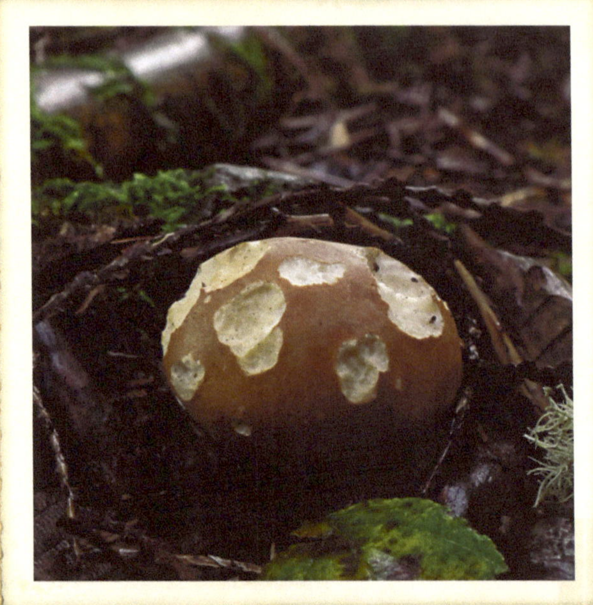

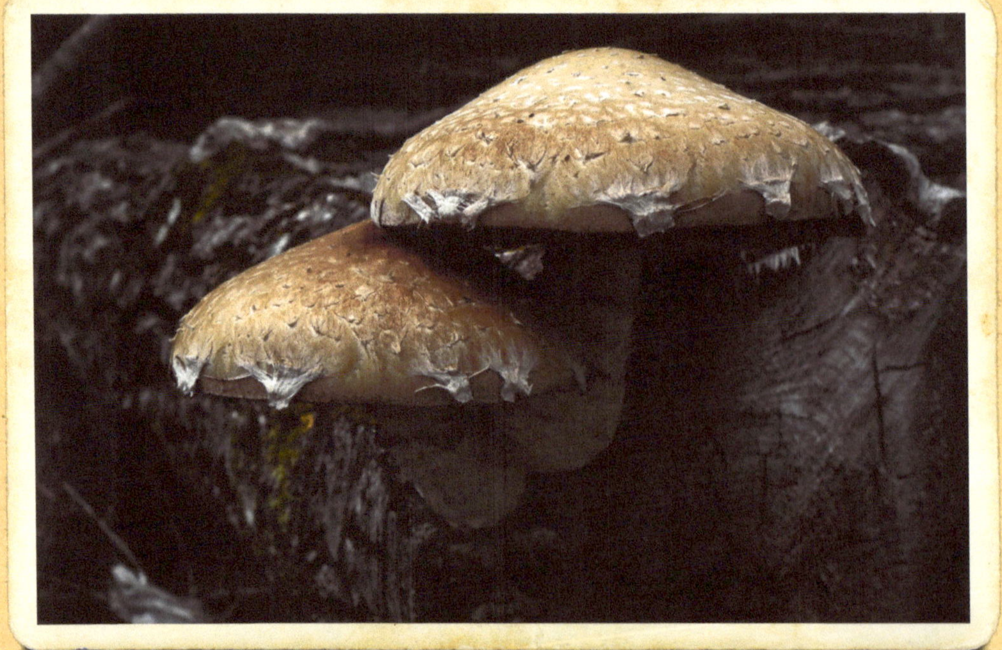

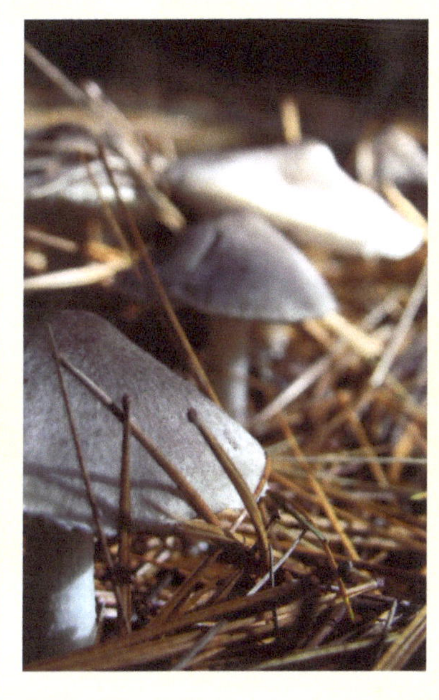

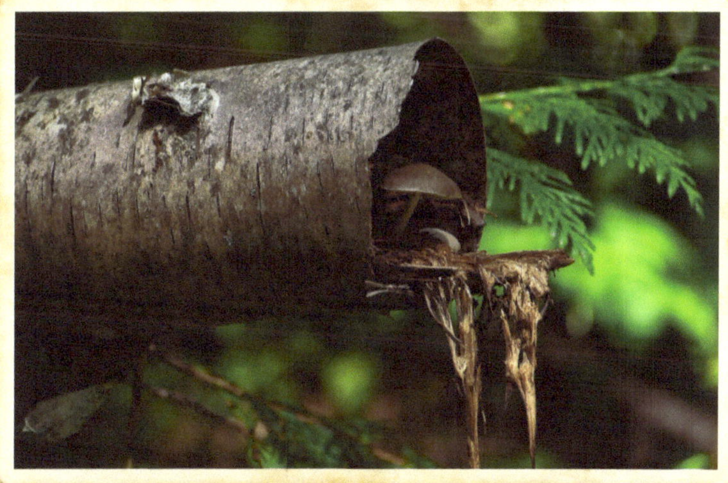

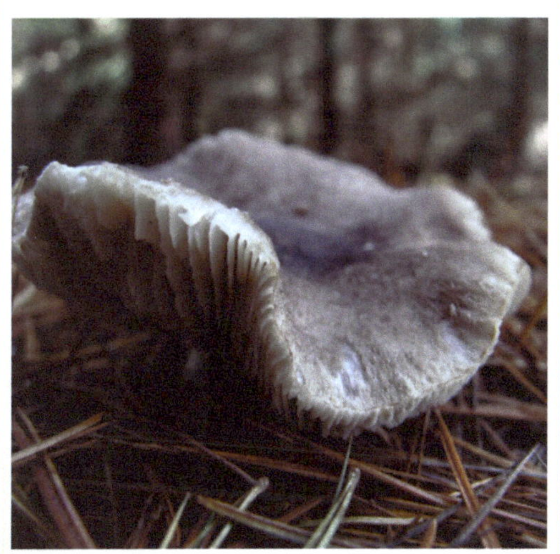

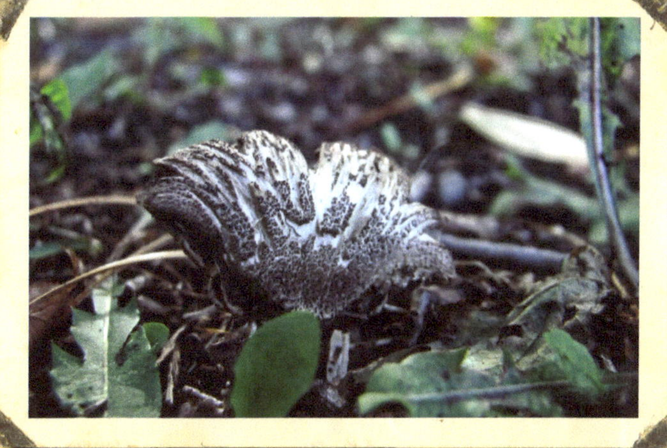

Thanks for reading my book. I hope you enjoyed both photos and poems.

Alex